LETTERS FROM
HOLLAND

BY

KAREL ČAPEK

TRANSLATED
FROM THE CZECH BY
PAUL SELVER

British Library Cataloguing-in-Publication Data
A catalogue record for this book is available from the
British Library

Karel Čapek

Karel Čapek was born in Malé Svatoňovice, the Austro-Hungarian Empire (now the Czech Republic) in 1890. He was expelled from school at the age of fifteen for founding an illegal students club, but graduated four years later with exceptional grades. After spending time at the Friedrich Wilhelm University in Berlin, and the Sorbonne of Paris, Čapek enrolled at the Charles University in Prague. He graduated in 1915 as a Master of Philosophy, and avoided the World War I conscription draft due to a problematic back.

In 1917, Čapek became a member of the board of editors of the *Narod* (*Nation*) magazine. Shortly afterwards he took up an editorship of the cultural section of the *Narodni listy* (the *National paper*), and the startup satirical weekly *Nebojsa* (*The Unafraid*).In the summer of 1920, Čapek published his first important work, a play called *R.U.R. (Rossum's Universal Robots)*. It was in this play that Čapek coined the now-popular word 'robot'. Throughout the twenties, having developed a strong aversion to nationalism and totalitarianism, he continued to pen politically influenced works, including the hugely popular *Ze života hmyzu* (*Pictures from the Insects' Life*) (1922), and *Krakatit* (1922), which predicts the development of nuclear weaponry.

During the thirties, Čapek's work began to focus on the threat of fascist dictatorships. His *Talks with T. G. Masaryk* was a bestseller (Masaryk was the first President of Czechoslovakia), and his anti-Nazi plays, *Bílá nemoc* (*The White Disease*) (1937) and *Matka* (*The Mother*) (1938) were also extremely popular. In 1938, despite the fact that the Nazi Gestapo had named him Czechoslovakia's "public enemy number two," Karel Čapek refused to leave his homeland. He died of pneumonia on Christmas Day of 1938.

Today, Čapek is considered one of the pioneers of European political science-fiction, and a forerunner to authors such as George Orwell and Ray Bradbury.

Contents

National Types

It is, of course, only fit and proper if the first thing I do on returning from the Netherlands is to describe and draw for you some typical Dutch faces. Now as regards the burgomasters, councillors, pundits

and other bigwigs, I must refer you to Flinck, de Keyser, Troost, Elias, Rembrandt, Sandrart and other Dutch masters of the seventeenth century, for since then the Dutch have not changed markedly in appearance, except that they no longer wear ruffs, bandoliers, cuirasses and other martial paraphernalia. But if you are more anxious to see some typical faces of old Dutch sailors, Calvinists and farmers, I beg to inform you that they can still be met with here and there; I myself saw one specimen of each at Utrecht, in the railway station at Gouda and in a tram at Leiden respectively, and I was delighted to come across that freak of nature which is known as a national type.

On Becoming Acquainted with Foreign Countries

In the majority of cases the modern traveller traverses foreign countries in a direction which, so to speak, runs counter to the course of history. Usually it is the chief railway station of the chief city which forms the starting-point of his investigations; not until later, and then slowly and little by little, does he arrive at the more and more ancient features of a place, such as cathedrals, ancient works of art and the Jews of Amsterdam, until right at the very end of his trip he discovers the actual voice of the earth, as represented by the mooing of piebald cows or the creaking wheels of a windmill. Accordingly, as a rule his first impression is that, on the whole, all regions of the world are alike (except for the confounded currencies), and then his final impression is apt to be that the regions of the world are infinitely various and lovely; but usually he does not arrive at this conclusion until it is too late, when he is getting back into the train at the chief railway station of the chief city and is slowly beginning to forget what he has seen.

Dutch Towns

Well now, to take things in their proper order, I must record that the first purely Dutch impression (apart from the green railway engines with brass helmets on their backs) consists of bricks. And windows. And bicycles in particular. And bricks and windows in particular. These bricks form the local colour of Holland: a green landscape containing cottages built of tiny red bricks with white seams, cottages with large bright windows, and a landscape with brick pathways along which bicycles scorch from one cottage to another, and these cottages, apart from the bricks, consist largely of windows, just windows, clean and large, with white frames, and most varied subdivisions and dimensions. For let me tell you that Dutch builders attach the greatest importance to windows; a wall's a wall, but a window is an aperture, a plastic affair which can be larger or smaller or broader or higher, and this, apparently, almost satisfies the individualistic needs of this country.

And then those bicycles. I have seen various things in my time, but never have I seen

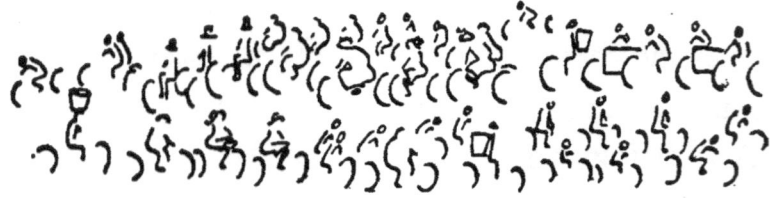

so many bicycles as for instance, in Amsterdam; they are no mere bicycles, but a sort of collective entity; shoals, droves, colonies of bicycles, which rather suggest the teeming of bacteria or the swarming of infusoria or the eddying of flies. The best part of it is when a policeman holds up the stream of bicycles to let pedestrians get across the street, and then magnanimously leaves the road open once more; a regular swarm of cyclists dashes forward, headed by a number of speed champions, and away they pedal, with the queer unanimity of dancing gnats. Experts on local conditions assert that at the present time there are close on two and a half million bicycles in the Netherlands, which means that there is one bicycle for every three inhabitants, including babies, sailors, the royal family and inmates of workhouses. I haven't counted them, but my impression was that the actual number is just a trifle bigger. I was told that all you have to do is to take your seat on a bicycle and it goes along by itself. That'll give you an idea of how smooth and straight the country is.

I saw nuns on bicycles and farmers on bicycles leading cows. People eat snacks on bicycles and take their children and their dogs for rides on bicycles, and courting couples go pedalling along, arm in arm, on bicycles, towards a blissful future; a nation on bicycles, in fact. When the bicycle has become a national habit to such an extent as that, we may well consider what effect it is likely to have on the national character. Personally I should say that:

(1) A man on a bicycle gets used to looking after himself and not getting mixed up with somebody else's bicycle.

(2) He waits for his opportunity and starts pedalling away the instant he gets the tiniest ration of elbow-room.

(3) He goes dashing along without having to exert himself overmuch, and without making the least fuss about it.

(4) Even when he sometimes rides in pairs or in a crowd, a man on a bicycle is more isolated and self-centred than a pedestrian.

(5) A bicycle brings about a kind of equality and uniformity among people.

(6) It teaches them to rely on the force of inertia.

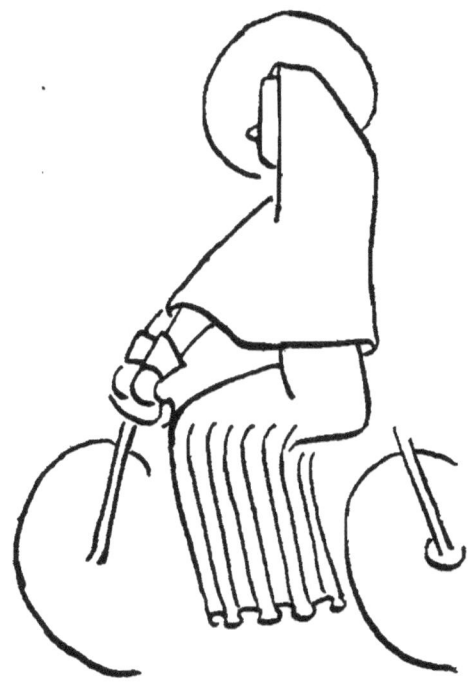

(7) And it fosters in them a sense of peace and quietness, such as is associated with cotton-wool.

The above opinions about bicycles are more favourable than what I really think about them; and now that they cannot get their own back on me, I don't mind declaring quite openly that I didn't like them, because to my mind it is somewhat unnatural for a man to be sitting and stepping forward at the same time. The practice of stepping forward

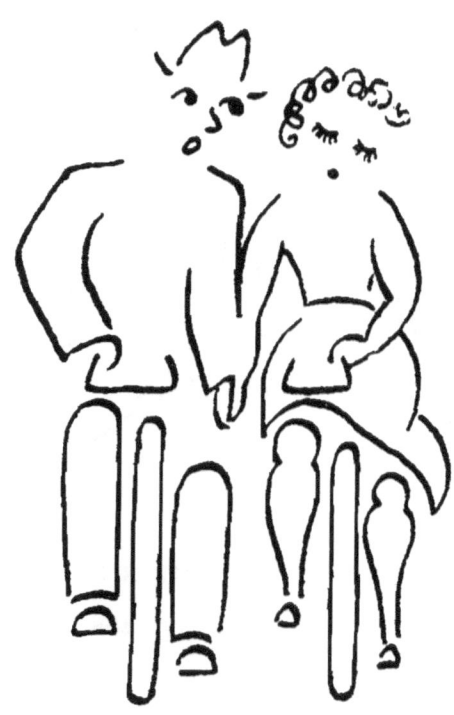

while seated can ultimately affect the pace of a nation's development. It becomes possible to tread slowly and nevertheless to get along quickly. You realize this when you see how far the Dutch have gone, although they tread

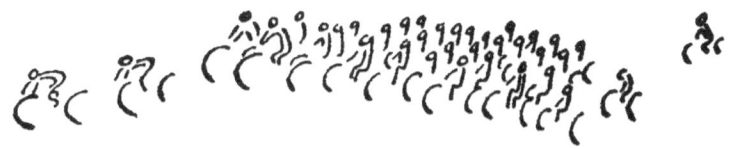

at about the same rate as a slow-motion film. But I, arm-swinging pedestrian that I am, will not interfere with their bicycles; let every nation follow its star by the methods which it understands.

There is one other conspicuous feature of the Dutch streets, viz. dogs. They have no muzzles and the consequence is that they keep on laughing almost out loud; nor do they quarrel or bite or growl at each other with that Central European touchiness; which only shows that freedom without a muzzle does not cause either dogs or human beings to go to the dogs, but is a paramount gift of God. Amen.

Grachts and Canals

Now this is the way of it: where we have streets between the houses, in Holland there is merely water; this is known as a gracht, and when the water flows from town to town it is a canal. And this restful water is not bordered with an embankment and a parapet, but with tall, restful trees and restful frontages of houses with shiny windows; and all of it is restfully mirrored in the water.

We are told that these grachts are really waterways, and that in olden times the Dutch used to carry goods on them all over the town. I do not propose to contradict this; for from time to time a boat with churns of milk or a cargo of flowers does, as a matter of fact, float staidly and restfully along them. But from the look of things I should be inclined to say that in olden times the Dutch built their towns of houses and water chiefly because in that way they could produce two towns at a single blow, so to speak: one on top and the other mirrored in the water. As, owing to the size of their country, they could not broaden out very much, they doubled

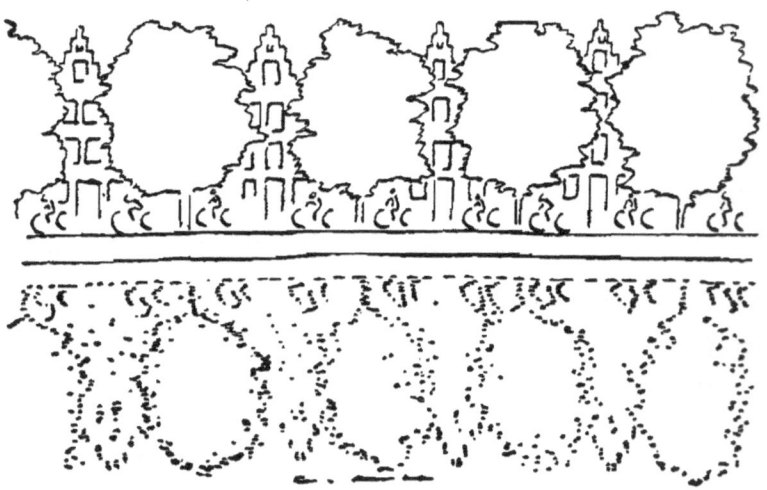

their dimensions vertically: by reflection in the water. As, on their sand, they could not to any extent stretch upwards, they simply reversed the process and produced a looking-glass effect downwards. It is the people who live on top, restfully and staidly; underneath, it is their shadows which move, even more restfully and staidly. I should not wonder if the surface of the grachts still reflected the shadows of people from bygone centuries, men in broad ruffs and women in mob caps. You see, these grachts are very old and consequently somehow unreal. The towns appear to be standing, not on the earth, but on their own reflections; these highly respectable streets appear to emerge from bottomless depths of dreams; the houses appear to be intended as houses and, at the same time, as reflections of houses.

There are bustling grachts with boats, big and small, floating along them, and there are grachts overgrown with a green coating of water-weed; there are shabby grachts which smell of swamp and fish, and high-class grachts which are privileged to reflect in full

lustre the frontages of patrician houses; there
are holy grachts in which churches are
mirrored, and dingy, lack-lustre canals in
which not even the light of heaven is reflected. There are the grachts in Delft, in
which red cottages are mirrored, and the
grachts in Amsterdam, in which the black
and white gables of tall buildings occupied
by shipping firms view themselves, and the
grachts in Utrecht, cut deep into the earth,
and tiny, derelict grachtlets which look as
if no human foot (shod with a boat) has
ever stepped on them, and grachts, now
filled in, of which only the name has been
left.

But the most grachtish effect of all is produced when towards evening the chimes
from the steeples are shed over the darkened
canals. They are like heavy drops resound-
ing on the dark and peaceful surface of the
water. You might almost think that these
pious chimes had been pouring down and
mingling together for hundreds and hundreds

of years, and thus produced these restful grachts.

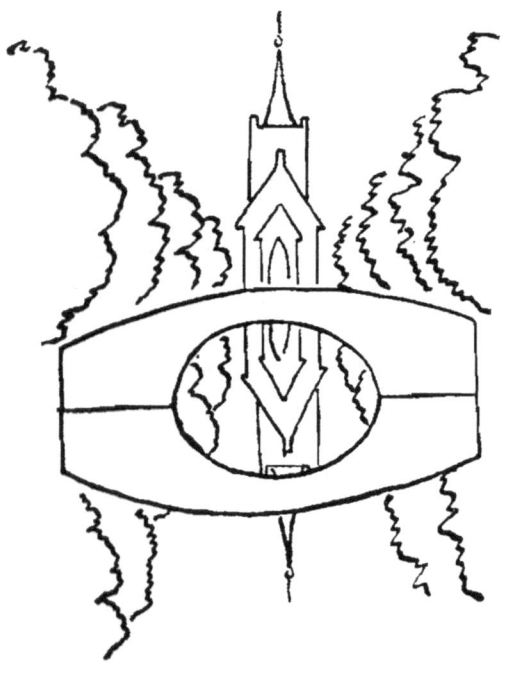

Old Towns

They are all alike, whether their name be Delft or Gouda or Leiden: a girdle of quiet waters and old brick cathedrals with timber vaultage like the bulging hull of a merchant vessel, and showy town halls, some large, some less so, decorated with all the diaper-work which betokens an ostentatious and wealthy bourgeoisie, and impressive public weigh-houses, and turreted gates, and fish markets, and venerable universities, and memorial houses, in which a Count of Orange or some such person was murdered at some time or other, and quiet little streets without any history, which themselves form a fragment of, say, the sixteenth or seventeenth centuries and drowse timelessly behind their slumbering strip of canal.

And these houses generally lean over like the tower of Pisa, for they are built on sand; sometimes they are only about four feet wide, because they are supported by posts, and in this country of water and sand every inch of firm soil is very precious; to save space, the upper floors are reached, not by a staircase, but by a narrow, breakneck arrangement like a ladder leading to a hen-roost, and that is why the furniture has to be carried in through the windows, because on this apology for a staircase such a proceeding would prove unsuccessful; and that is why these houses are provided with gables from which ropes and pulleys can be suspended, and that is why these windows are so wide; and, to wind up with, that is why the Dutch are such staid people and do not gad about, for once anybody has managed to climb home on such a breakneck contraption, he is glad not to have to crawl down again, but can stay where he is and sit by his shiny window and peep into a

slanty strip of looking-glass to see what is
happening in the street (but nothing is happening there, because everyone is at home,
peeping into a slanty strip of mirror and not
gadding about)—that only shows you how
is everything bound up with the nature of the
soil. That is why the architecture of Dutch
towns has not changed fundamentally in the

course of centuries; such present-day places as Oud or Dudok only had to take the same neat, home-made, smooth bricks and the same large, clean windows, of which old Delft or Utrecht is built, the only difference being that they had a trifle more room for

adding new suburbs; but in other respects these new streets are just as shapely and just as modern as the old ones mirrored in the ancient grachts. Just peep through the half-opened doors into the living-rooms; to this very day the glimpses you will catch are like pictures by old Vermeer van Delft.

And having said van Delft, I may as well also say van Gogh. You get quite a different idea of van Gogh's pigments, when you see the pigments of the Dutch earth, the colours almost as clear as enamel, the brick-reds, the lush green pastures, the yellow sand, the brightly coloured facias and sign-boards, the fondness for clear colours sparkling in the clarity of the air: all this was devised by van Gogh from his native Holland, for the colours of France are quite different, poplar-silvery and bluish and opal-grey; no sooner had this Dutchman felt a little of the heat from a more southern sun, than he was in his best form.

Towns built on piles: this has imparted yet another aspect to Dutch towns. It came about in this way: when the town was to be built, a sheet of water was taken, it was enclosed by a dyke and drained off, and then houses were built there. Dutch towns have not grown in a tentacular way, but in compact zones; that is why they have no outskirts, they do not straggle like patches of rash, but squat nice and neat on a green meadow. I might almost say that where the cathedral ends, the cow begins, and vice versa; without the slightest warning you are confronted with a vermilion township on top of a green pasture; and this is a delightful and purely Dutch affair.

From Town to Town

And there are straight highroads lined with old trees and leading from town to town, just as in olden times when

Hobbema was alive, alongside the highroads and canals, an endless vista of canals, endlessly bisecting the flat landscape; canals with barges, canals with sailing boats, canals with water-lilies in bloom; and on the skyline avenues of poplars and rows of stocky willows, families of windmills and church steeples; canals taking the place of hedges, canals taking the place of roads, canals taking

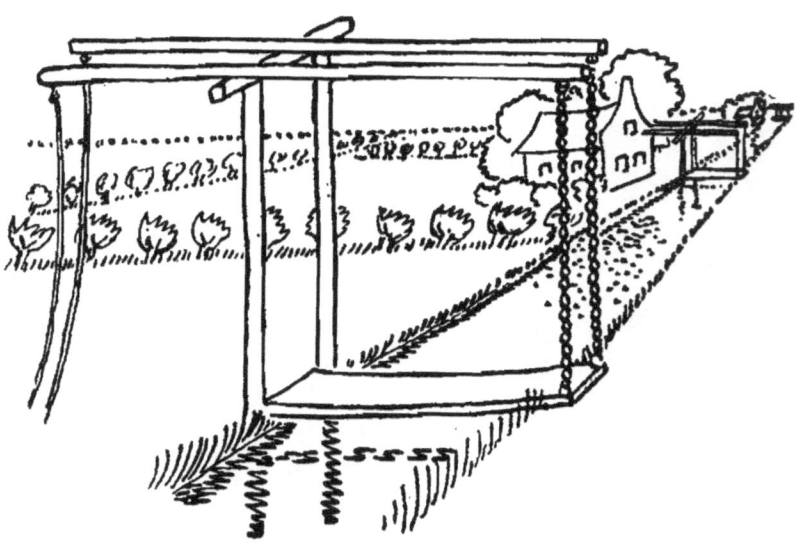

the place of fences, canals taking the place of footpaths. The farmer loads a barge with hay, takes a boat to go and milk the cows, inspects his field while standing in a wherry and pushes off with a pole; in a standing posture he proceeds from place to place; I cannot help wondering whether he does his ploughing and reaping also while standing in his wherry. His house is surrounded, not by a fence but by a canal; instead of a gate just a drawbridge, and that's that.

There are straight canals leading from town to town; but these canals are not below the level of the ground, as elsewhere, but above it: the surface of the water is thus above the level of the ground, the water flows on top and people trudge along down below, with boats sailing almost above their heads. But these people have complete confidence in their dykes and their water; it is perhaps this confidence which keeps the dykes in their place. And then, too, you must bear in mind that this water, unlike other water, flows uphill; from the low-lying land and its canals and gulleys it is pumped upwards into the rivers and waterways; and that is why these canals are lined with regular avenues of wind-mills, which do not grind corn, but water;

they draw it from the gulleys to the canals, from the canals to the waterways, from the waterways to the rivers and from the rivers the water then flows of its own accord, so to speak, *per vias naturales.*

To-day, however, most of these windmills no longer wave their arms and no longer grind water, but serve merely as an emblem of Holland; and the water is shifted by electricity.

Man and Water

Well now, with my own eyes I have seen how Holland is being produced. It is the same as with their towns: you take a bit of sea, fence it in and pump it out; and at the bottom is left a deposit to which a respectable slice of Europe,

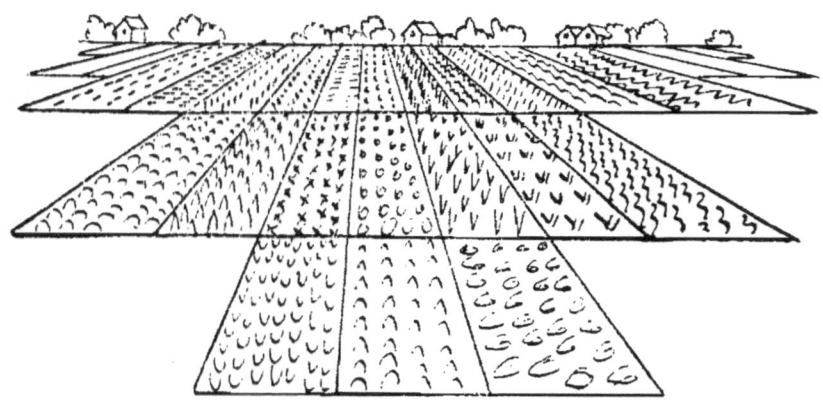

by means of its rivers, supplies its best swampy soil, and the sea its fine sand; the

Dutchman drains it and sows grass there, the cows feed on it, the Dutchman milks them, and thus makes cheese, which at Gouda or Alkmaar is sold to England; and this, incidentally, is a suggestive example of metabolism.

What used to be this deposit is called polder and can be recognized by its exceedingly tidy, lush and pleasing appearance, and by the fact that there is nothing whatever about it which recalls so stirring an event as the struggle between man and water. For one thing, these renowned polders are unusually rectilinear; when the Dutchman set about producing his land, he did so in a properly human manner, that is, with the aid of a foot rule, just as when planks are being sawn up. Crooked is the history of man, but rectilinear are his works.

I saw the operations connected with the draining of the Zuider Zee. Imagine a real sea, which could be fitted in somewhere between Oldham, Stoke, Derby and Sheffield, let us say; a sea with storms and steamers and all the maritime appurtenances. On one side a dyke is built, some eighteen miles long, but

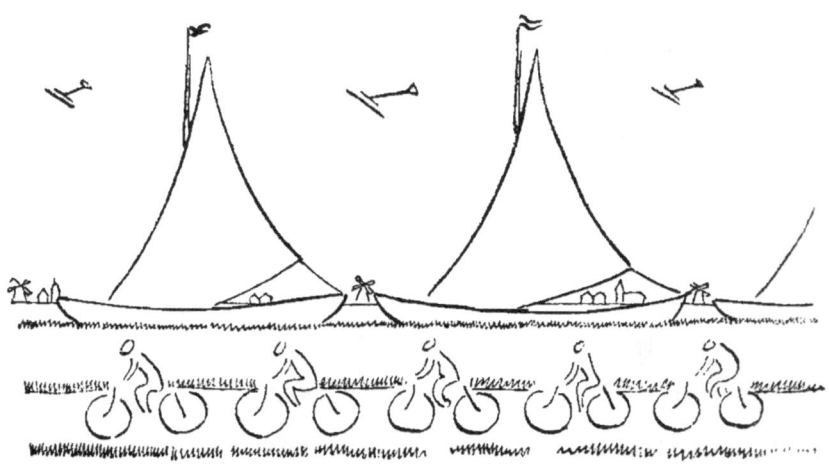

it is the merest dykelet against that huge stretch of water; on this dykelet midget trains carry Swedish granite, getting a yard or so further each day; and when this is finished, a river will be made in the middle of this sea, and an island in the middle of this river, and then the sea will be drained and after thirty years or so piebald cows will make their appearance.

Man and Water

Yes, but already they are getting worried as to how the bottom of the sea is to be shared out. The farmer in Friesland will not leave his pastures and the bulb-grower in the polders of Haarlem will be unwilling to part from his flower-beds; it will take decades before the salty pastures are turned into dry and fertile soil. But the midget trains go puffing away along the toy dyke; and day by day the Dutch nation is working at a task which will provide only the next generation but one with orbs of cheese and tulip bulbs.

And where there are no dykes the seashore is simply woven from wattles to prevent the heaped-up sand from slipping into the water. Just imagine that only wicker-work and a sandy parapet divide water and land; if the wicker-work gave way, the sea would flow into the clogs of half the population of Holland. That is why so many stocky willows grow there, to provide material from which the shores can be woven.

On the Beach

B ut before the land actually comes into
contact with the sea, it arches its back
a little in the guise of straggling hill-
ocks and ridglets; these are the old dunes,
drift-sand cast up by the sea, a small-scale
wilderness which fringes the land of the polders; first there are shrubs and copses, and
then only just a little grass, and after that
nothing but heaped-up sand; and in it the

continual sea breeze sets astir only tough wisps of fescue grass or sedge; please note that this shaky herbage is sown here over and over again; please note also that these parched stalks fulfil the important purpose of keeping the dunes in place by means of their roots, and thus protecting the shores of Holland.

And at the foot of the sand-dunes stretches the soft sand of the beaches washed by the rise and fall of the tide, and strewn with shells; seaside resorts, big and small, and bathing-places, one after another, extending as far as the eye can reach and even farther; arrays of tents and basket-chairs, forming an encampment for whole families, children at play in the sand, the whole nation basking in the mild sunshine; and then nothing but the sea, grey and harsh-toned, a steamer sweeping along full-tilt from the Hook van Holland or thereabouts, the moist breath of the ocean, the smell of fish; also much sparkle and mirror-effects. Man alive, this is a place where you could spend hours looking at the horizon and sifting the warm sand between your fingers; you'll probably never take a

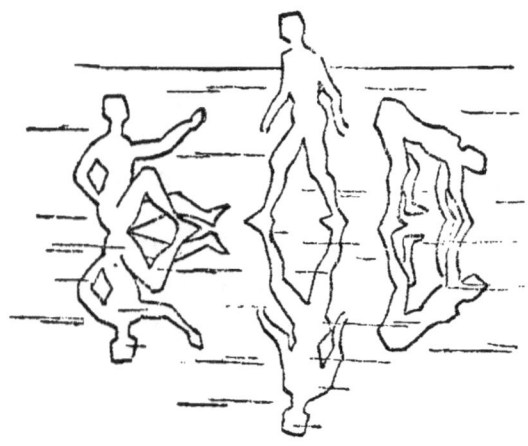

trip over there any more, but never mind, the world is wide.

And I saw, I don't know whether it was in Nordwijk or Katwijk or elsewhere, a Mass Attack of Jellyfish; the whole beach was densely strewn with their transparent, pulpy mortal remains which resembled the dung of ghost-cows; and when I crept into the sea, I could not keep clear of the soft and phlegmy touch of their feelers; I beat a retreat, appalled

and regretful; that day the sea was lovelier
than it had ever been except on three previous

occasions in the geological history of the
world. And one night I saw the sea all phos-
phorescent; on the peak of a wave a green
sparkle darted out and shed itself like a flash
of lightning which is dissolving in water;
there were moments when the whole expanse
of the sea was ablaze with a cold phosphor-
escence which rolled towards the shore and

was quenched there. I may add that I have witnesses to prove this.

But what is loveliest of all is the Sunday sea, the democratic sea, fringed with children and enclosed by the trenches which they have dug and the ramparts which they have built of warm sand; the odd thing is that the children's sea is just as big as the sea of the ocean liners.

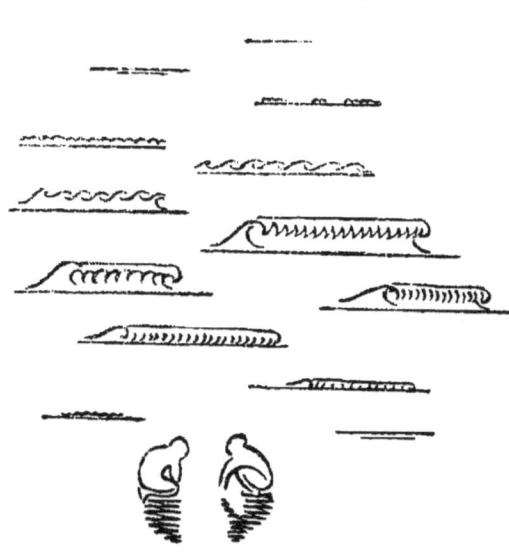

Harbours

I must confess that I am a wretched land-lubber; perhaps that is the very reason why I am always enchanted by the sight

of a harbour, even if it consists only of a dark bollard with a dinghy moored to it. In a certain respect I prefer harbours which contain fishing smacks, boats with masts and spars and sails and rigging; for these are the ships of dreams, sailing vessels bound on adventurous voyages.

'Furl the jib!' shouted the captain. 'Six men to the pumps! Cut away the rigging!' Whither have ye departed, old brigs and sloops and three-masters equipped with culverins, and likewise ye drunken captains brandishing the cat-o'-nine-tails and stingily dealing out to the disgruntled crew their

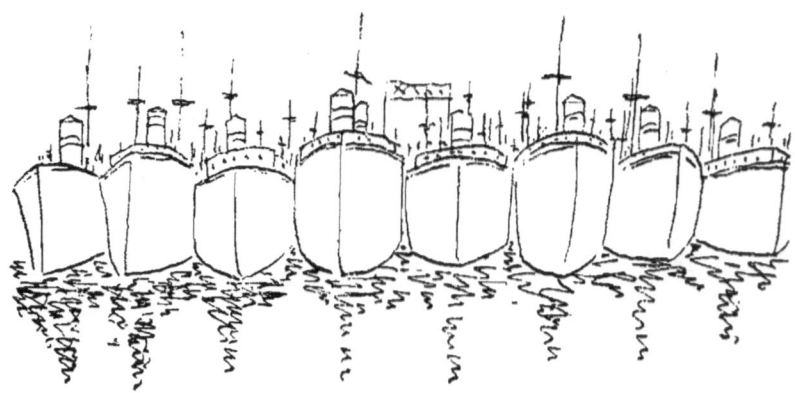

rations of mildewed ship's-biscuit and water with weevils in it? Of these gorgeous things of the past, all that is left are the herring-trawlers with red sails which look white when seen from a distance, with festoons of nets and the crew in breeches of monumental size stolidly pottering about; but here, too, it is pleasant to loiter, lolling against the parapet, and to spit expertly into the dark water and to ponder profoundly and in zig-zags like the outlines of those masts.

Furl the sails, my lads, and coil up the ropes; you haven't much of a chance, with all these brigs and schooners here in the waters of the Yssel or Maas, in the tidal basins of Rotterdam, in the docks and vaarts of Amsterdam; you haven't much of a chance among these pot-bellied craft laden with corn, these paunchy boats full of coal, these tankers, elevators, silos and derricks and gang-planks and dredgers and white liners from Java and India and Guiana, and stocky motor boats and pilots' steam launches,

among these blowzy trollops of cargo-boats
which hobnob with the scum of every blessed
harbour in the world, and grey ironclads, and

sluggish tug-boats; you haven't much of a
chance, my good man, with your landlubber
vocabulary among these mooing ocean-cows
and elephants and swarthy pigs, in this vast
ocean-stable, where the animals snort and
feed and sleep, where bells ring and chains
clank; look at those brown Malays with the

flower-patterned turbans; look at that vis-
cous, oily water: gold from every quarter of
the globe is dissolved in it.

And then they talk about a small country.
A tiny land which has its vessels in all the
seven seas. One of the small fry among
countries, but one which is being suckled at
the bulging udders of Earth; listen here to it
drinking its fill in noisy gulps.

And at dusk, in the byways near the harbour, lights are lit behind drawn crimson
curtains, mechanical music begins to blare,
and blowzy wenches drift forth into the dark
streams of night; old, weather-beaten tramp-
steamers waiting for their cargo.

Highways and Byways

There's no getting away from it, if you really want to know what a country's like, you must leave the train and proceed on Shanks' pony, by bicycle, car, motor-bus, boat or scooter; for railways cut through a landscape like a scalpel, so to speak, while highroads and rivers pass across it organically, by routes which, for centuries, life itself has traversed. The landscape which you see from the train is monotonous and devoid of charm; but saunter through it by other routes, and you will discover trees, people, villages, traces of history and possibly even the soul of the place.

When you are touring the Dutch countryside, however, you had better not be in too much of a hurry; for at every moment a bridge is raised under your very nose to let a boat pass through with its cargo of salad or butter, and to enable the genius loci to whisper to you: 'There's plenty of time, plenty of time; why, my dear sir, I've been here for some six hundred years.'

O, Dutch polders, what a pity that I missed the season for tulips and narcissi and tazettas and all that makes the Dutch fields so lovely; so far I had seen only bulbs being dug up, just as potatoes are hoed in our country; but at least I saw gladioli in bloom and fields of larkspur, roods of golden lilies, bushels of roses, acres of hardy annuals, hides of nursery gardens and flower-beds and forcing-grounds; I saw regular landscapes under glass, miles of hothouses, wholesale production of flora, a blossom industry, endless vegetation factories; truckfuls of flowers, shiploads of flowers, aeroplanes with flowers heading full-tilt for England. And in the houses, windows overflowing with flowers, a nosegay on every

table, a flower-seller at every corner, boats laden with flowers on the grachts. A hectic yield of roses, lupines, water-lilies, sweet-peas, Siberian gladioli. Rose gardens covered with a froth of red, yellow, bronze, icy-white roses. Bouquets of azaleas, thickets of rhodo-dendrons, jungles of ilex and bullace.

And the prettiest little gardens in the world are those of the Dutch cottages; quite tiny, as

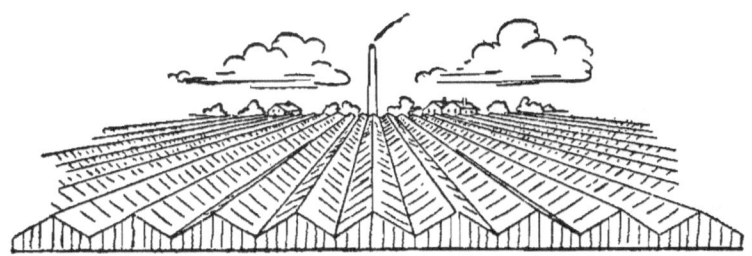

fresh as fresh can be from the frequent showers, teeming with silvery, golden and purple leaves, bestrewn with a bounty of blossoms; the smallest of terraces, with pillows of orach and alyssum, a pool no bigger than the palm of your hand with red waterlilies floating on it, a little coppice of bar-

berry, midget woods of golden juniper and blue cypresses. Well (quoth the envious gardener within me), it's easy enough for *them*; if *I* had such soft, peaty soil, if *I* had the benefit of all those spells of moist weather, if *I* had such a mild winter and these supplies of seedlings and the cash and so forth, why, hang it all, don't you think I'd have everything all a-growing and a-blowing?

Yes, gardener, you would; but there's something more than that about these Dutch flowers. My good fellow, these nosegays show the results of five hundred years of gardening work; just look how dignified, how—what's the word I want?—yes, how *well-groomed* they are; there's no getting over a few hundred years' start in any sphere of activity. Then, too, I must add that there's another peculiar item which counts, and that is, Dutch light.

Dutch Light

I can't very well sketch Dutch light for you, it is so pure and transparent that you can see every outline and detail to the very edge of the world; that is why those old painters used to elaborate their pictures to the minutest details so plainly and with an almost microscopic accuracy; it is the dewy air in Holland which made this possible. And then, too, Dutch light imparts a peculiar purity to colours; they are extremely clear, but they are neither hectic nor gaudy; they are like a fresh flower beneath a drop of dew. They are pure and cool. I just mention this to show you that light has a great influence on art and flowers and also on a girl's complexion.

Pastorale

Holland implies water. Holland implies flower-beds. Holland implies pastures. The green polder between the canals with piebald cows on it, or the cows may be black with white heads, or black

with a white girdle and a blue mouth, or with black and white spots like kidney beans; cows with rugs on the backs to keep them dry; herds either grazing, dreaming or chewing the cud; cows as dignified and well-bred as dowagers, beeves who are full-blown dignitaries with pedigrees, regular patricians among cows. As far as the eye can see, nothing but a velvety meadow studded with piebald herds. That is the real Holland.

That is the real Holland; a green polder between canals and on it herds of horses, massive Frisian geldings, flat-nosed and broad-shouldered, with legs like pillars and fluttering manes. They are fenced in only by a canal, which cannot be seen for the high grass; it looks as if they could run off to Utrecht or Zwolle, as if the broad stretch of country belonged to them, the massive lords of the free realm of horses. That is the real Holland.

The green polder between the canals with white sheep in it, the curly-haired souls of the

righteous on the green meadows of paradise. The green polder between the canals with black piglets grunting on it to show their approval. The green polder between the canals with hundreds and hundreds of chickens on it. Or shaggy goats. And nowhere a sign of a human being; that is the real Holland.

Pastorale

It is not until the approach of evening that a man comes sailing up in a wherry, sits down

on a footstool and milks the stately cows. In the west the sky takes on a golden tinge, somewhere in the distance a steamer hoots, and that is all; no herdsman cooees, there is no tinkle of bells from the cows returning to their byres, and even the man on the footstool is completely tongue-tied.

A boat slips quietly along the canal laden with churns of milk; a regular convoy of lorries dashes along the highroad laden with churns of milk; and trains puff towards the towns laden with churns of milk. And when that is over, there is complete stillness; no cur yelping, no cow mooing in the byre, no horse knocking its hoof against the partition of its crib, nothing; only somewhere on the horizon beyond the dark and mute polders of sleeping herds the lighthouses silently rummage in the darkness with the feelers of their rays.

That is the real Holland.

Old Holland

Besides the real Holland there is what is known as Old Holland; but please don't confuse the two: you see, the real Holland is mostly old, but Old Holland is mostly not real.

Thus, there are fishing villages which do not make their living from fish, but from trippers and painters (especially of the low-brow kind); in these old villages they go in for old houses, old ships, old costumes and old fishermen with garlands of whiskers and enormous breeches. On the island of Vollendam they go in for the most roomy trousers, sheepskin headgear, with striped petticoats and winged bonnets for the women; on the island of Marken the people make their living

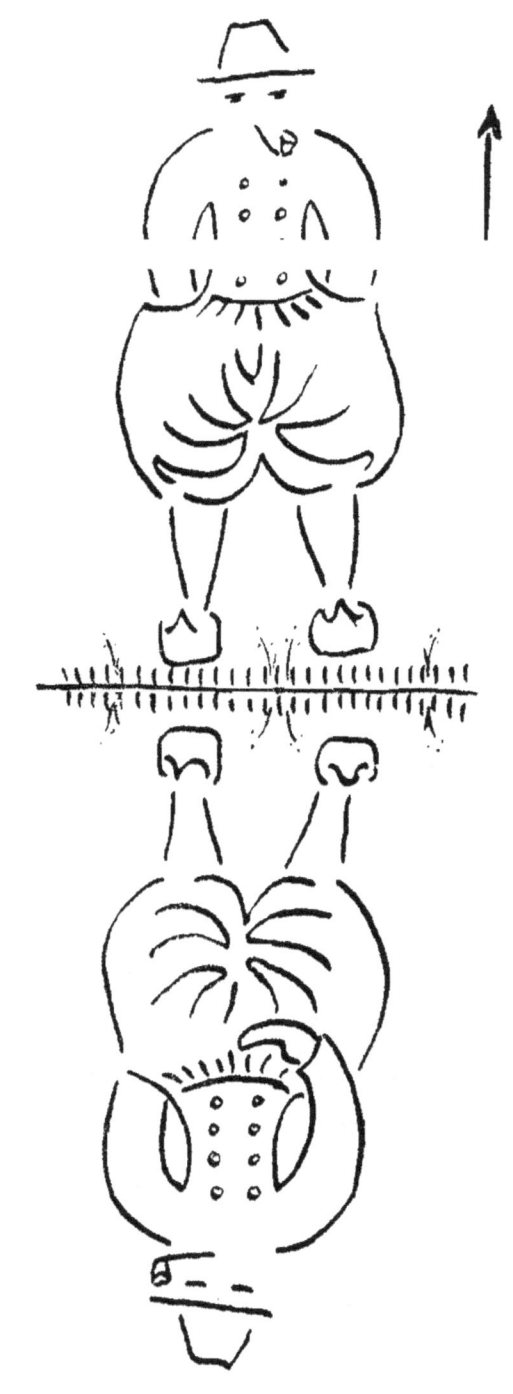

from short, wide breeks, gaudy bodices and dishevelled hair; in return for this they receive a government grant and sell clogs, picture postcards, lace and other souvenirs to the trippers who get across on boats, where they are packed like sardines, and take photographs of the old women and children in the old costumes (half a gulden per person), slink into the cottages (entrance free, sale of picture postcards)—in fact it's a highly romantic business; the people here speak mostly English, German and French.

I don't want to try and make you think that I have a sensitive soul, but I'm bound to say I felt a little uncomfortable to see the people selling themselves to trippers who were like so many *voyeurs*. I slipped away to take a snapshot of some fishing boats (in case I might ever want to try my hand at a dreamship for myself); from one of the boats emerged a fisherman in fancy dress and a towering rage, who went for me with a broom: *No you don't! Nobody's going to photo-*

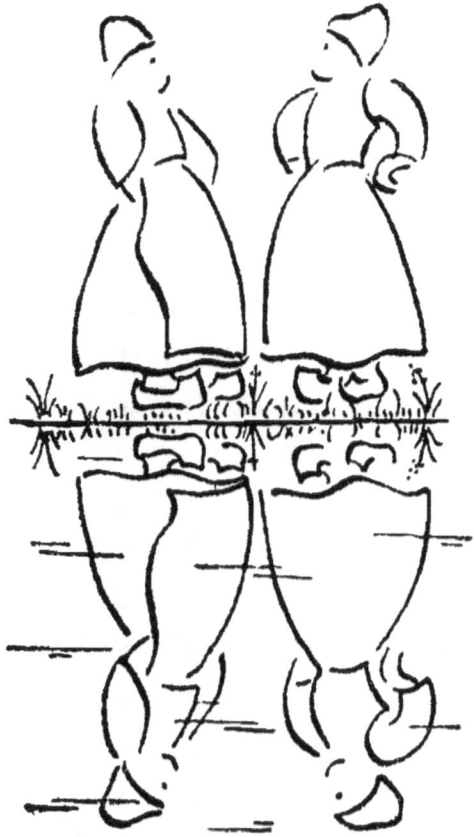

graph me! I felt much relieved. This man at
least was real.

And that reminds me, fellow countrymen,
that we too are faced with this problem; we
too would like to preserve, at least here and

there, some specimens of our typical native costumes and dwellings; in our country, too, the suggestion has been made that folklore should receive a government grant, as if it were a sort of national park. I shall be sorry for every wooden cottage which disappears, for every embroidered sleeve which is no longer worn; but I wouldn't like to see Slovakia imitating the example of places like Marken and Vollendam. It is below the dignity both of folklore and the people.

Old Holland

But there is still the Old Holland which
does not look as if it were a stuffed specimen

or rigged out in fancy dress; here servant
girls still pass to and fro in Zeeland mob
caps; here clogs are still worn in the fields,
not because it is folklore, but because clogs
are really small boats for walking through
water. There are still *béguinages* and poor-
law asylums and almshouses as Josef Israels
painted them; nowhere do you see so many
old people as in Holland, the public benches
are filled with them enjoying the warmth of
the mild sunshine and spared the evils of a

lonely old age. This Christian kindliness to
the old is also a part of the real Old Holland.

Old Holland

As regards national music, it consists mainly of the concertina. This is a most healthy instrument, because it tremendously promotes the broadening of the shoulders.

Modern Holland

B ut if you were to ask me what I liked most of all in Holland, I should unbosom myself without any long reflection, and say: the houses. Also the cows. Also the harbours. Also Vermeer van Delft. Also the flowers. Also the grachts. Also the sky. But as I said houses first of all, let it be houses.

I do not know what sort of position the women have in Holland, but I think that it must be (to use the expert phraseology) a preponderant one, for the cleanliness which prevails throughout Holland is downright feminine. I do not mean that they have petticoat-rule, but there can be no doubt that they have mop-rule. In England I was surprised to see how the people there fortify their houses, turning them into strongholds against the street by means of a railing, a front garden and, on top of all that, a screen of ivy. In Holland I was still more surprised to see how the people link house with street: in front of the windows an unenclosed garden and the broad, shiny windows entirely uncovered, so that every passer-by can see the well-being and the model family life in the lamplight. A Dutch street is really an interior; it is nothing more or less than a passage used by a number of neighbours in common, and that is why it is so clean and tidy.

In Holland they build, not houses but streets; houses, at one remove, so to speak, are hardly more than internal fittings. They are cupboards and lockers for people to live in; they are dusted, too, with all the respect due to family furniture. And when you get inside them, there is nothing but windows and wide folding doors, the purpose of which is to make the limited space look ampler than

it is. And on the walls nothing but landscapes, as if they were windows peeping out
on to shrubberies and polders, windmills and
canals. Why, I'll be hanged if this isn't an old
Cuyp and here's an old van de Velde; here's
some old Delft china and this is empire pew-
ter; you see, it is not only the things, but the
families as well which are old.

And then there are the brand-new streets
and suburbs. While elsewhere they talk no
end about modern architecture, schemes of
town-planning, workmen's dwellings and
other features of progress, here miles and
miles of them have been carried out; and
some of these workmen's streets and suburbs
look very much the kind of thing that
you would imagine housing arrangements
to be a hundred years hence: extremely
wide streets with grass lawns for the
children, houses which are not merely
sunny, but downright radiant, festooned
with balconies, sheer glass and air. And
everywhere notices 'to let' or 'to be sold',

for these fine new suburbs are still half empty.

In its own way modern Holland sets an example for modern architects to copy: build purposefully, by all means; build to meet the needs of modern life, utilizing all the resources of housing, by all means; but at the same time, as a matter of course and with proper discrimination, remain true to the spirit of the country, tradition, national character or whatever you choose to call it. Modern Dutch architecture is very modern, but it is also very Dutch.

And here let us remark with a touch of envy: there's no getting over a few centuries' start in any sphere of human activity. Give us a few hundred years and you'll see what we can do.

Old Masters

Now I want to come to the point; now, I mean, I want to come to the Mauritshuis and the Rijksmuseum and all the rest of the picture galleries and collections and museums. In my time I've looked at heaps and heaps of the old Dutch painters and I've visited no end of galleries; sometimes I liked them, sometimes they pleased me only slightly, but it wasn't until I went to Holland that I really found my bearings among them.

They are sometimes called 'small masters', because for the most part they painted small pictures; but they painted these small pictures for the small houses and rooms which to this very day, still peep at the small streets and

grachts; no cathedral altars, no palace fres-
coes and canvases; please remember that
space had to be used charily here, in painting
as in other things.

And they are called 'small masters' also because they painted, not St. Sebastians and
Assumptions and Holy Families and Dianas
and Venuses, but the small things in life, such
as a slaughtered duck, a worthy uncle on the
mother's side, peasants at a beanfeast, cows
at pasture or a ship at sea. As regards the St.
Sebastians, just go and have a look inside the
Dutch cathedrals. Calvinism stripped them
of all idols, whether graven, carved or painted,
and left them as bare as vessels without a
cargo, high and dry on the beach; sculpture
hasn't got over this even yet, and painting
had to apply itself to earthly matters; hounded
out of the cathedrals, it found its way into the
kitchen, the tavern, the world of clodhop-
pers, shopkeepers, old ladies and charitable
societies, and made itself remarkably snug
and contented there. As regards the Dianas

and Venuses, it was perhaps Dutch puritan-
ism or perhaps also the Dutch climate which
kept them away; such damp and rheumaticky
surroundings are not exactly in the best interests of nudity.

And so, partly through lack of space,
partly as the result of the Reformation, there
arose a Dutch art which was secular, small-
scale and bourgeois. But I haven't yet come
to the point I wanted to make, and that is,
that the Dutch painter did not work standing
like Titian, or prone on a scaffolding, like
Michael Angelo, but sitting down. Being
seated, he took pains with his picture, rev-
elled in details, scanned things closely, fami-
liarly and without any feeling of remoteness.
Being seated, he arranged on his table flowers
or fish, a glass of wine, grapes, lobsters, mel-
ons and other things good to look at, and
then dallied with them on the canvas. Potter
painted his bull when he was looking upwards and hence sitting down; Vermeer van
Delft painted his figures from the angle of

vision which German photographers call
Bauchperspektive, and hence sitting down.
Brower and Ostade used to sit in country
inns. Jan Steen had his seat among the topers
and ladies of the town. Cuyp seated himself in
the open and painted landscapes. Ruisdael
sat at home and painted landscapes. Old
Breughel was the only one who looked at
things at all from above, but he was really a
Belgian.

Dutch art is the work of seated painters for
sedentary townsfolk; an urban art which
sometimes paints peasants, but does so with
the condescending banter of sedate urban
shopkeepers. They are fond of still-lifes.
They are fond of pictures which tell a story;
stories provide entertainment for sedentary
people. These pictures were not painted for
galleries where people walk about, but for
rooms where they sit down. Dutch art re-
vealed a new reality by betaking itself home
and sitting down there.

The world in which it sits is restful, talkative and easy-going, it is cosy, matter-of-fact, sociable and rather given to tittle-tattle; it notices the things nearest to it, and this is really how it reveals them; it observes at close quarters and with enjoyment. Make an excited man sit down; immediately he drops his heroics and all his grandiose posturings. Nobody can preach sitting down; all he can do is to talk. By sitting down permanently on its wicker footstool, Dutch art banished all high-flown heroics from itself and the world which it portrays; it began to look at things more from close quarters and more from below.

Until at last we come upon Rembrandt, an awesome and tragical figure, swathed in the dim and ruffled mantle of twilight.

VERMEER VAN DELFT

I will not enumerate to you all the goodly masters, both major and minor, who painted landscapes and genre-pictures and still-lifes and portraits; they have attractive names such

as Dou and Terboch, Hobbema, Cuyp and
Metsu and de Hoogh, Wouwerman, van der
Neer, van de Velde, van Goyen and lots
more. I should like to linger a little more
among them (seated, and pledging their
health in a podgy and clouded glass of wine)
but now my eyes are still full of that dazzling
purity which takes its name from the pleasing
town of Delft; the lustrous purity of Vermeer. A girl reading a letter, a kitchen-maid,
a lady in blue, a view of Delft; these are only
a few glimpses of the peaceful and homely
life, but nobody else has caught the clear, the
transparent, the what I might call dewy
Dutch light, the feminine quietude, the lum-
inous composure and the intimate sanctity of
a home which is fragrant with the smoothing
iron, with soap and with woman's presence.
Let the pilgrim hold his breath and walk on
tiptoe in front of these pictures, for strange,
solemn and almost uncanny is the secret of
purity.

FRANS HALS

And now you need no longer hold your breath and talk in undertones, for here is stuff for he-men. Just look at the fellow as painted by himself; sprawled out and befuddled, stout and burly, a roysterer in Sunday clothes, with a head which was not given to brooding, and a hand which did not toy with the brush but slapped it across the canvas with a rollicking, virile matter-of-factness and self-assurance which are little short of effrontery. A relentless master of his craft. He knocked these portraits off, with scarcely the flicker of a bleary eyelid; and he made things lifelike too; starchy pleats crackle, high-minded wives of burgesses breathe hard in their tight stays, worshipful town councillors snort, and the old master slung it almost savagely on to the canvas, probably because the bigwigs were not altogether to his liking. Genius of a downright physical character. One of those thoroughgoing, full-blooded

men whose sojourn in this world is cut short
by drink and apoplexy.

REMBRANDT

Rembrandt or the exception. It is true that
afterwards he was copied by others, by a
much larger school, in fact, than you probably supposed, but they failed to get at his
secret. It was a personal secret. It was the
conflict between a tragical romantic and the
world of staid burgesses. One of the first ro-
mantics in the world and he had to be born in
that bright, humdrum, shallow Holland, of all
places. They still show you his house on the
fringe of the Amsterdam ghetto. This is not
merely Rembrandt's address, but part and
parcel of his inner destiny. Flight from Pro-
testant restraint. Unhappiness and social
derangement. The search for darkness, the
search for the Orient. A man in whom
brooding, sensualism, effusiveness and stark
realism were strangely mingled. The warm
gloom of his pictures glimmers with gems

and the body's decay, the bearded heads of
Talmudists, and the moist eyes of Susanna.
The Son of Man and the countenance of man;
but chiefly and above all else, the troublous,
the dire, the mournful, the ineffable Soul of
man. The greatest irony which he encoun-
tered was that, judging from the number of
his satellites, he must have had quite a considerable success in his own country. Nevertheless he died in a state of bankruptcy; and
for two hundred and fifty years his next-of-
kin have, with all due formalities, been ap-
plying for the bankruptcy proceedings against
the painter Rembrandt Harmensz van Rijn to
be suspended.

Worthy folk from all over the world
piously throng in front of his pictures which
are fashioned of gloom and lustre; but these
pictures remain inscrutable. And the pilgrim
who desired to behold and to fathom the
secret of a small nation, at least from its art,
was confronted by an even queerer secret: the
riddle of a great artist.

A SMALL NATION

The thing is this: but for Rembrandt, the pilgrim's final impression would have been that the small-scale happiness of a small nation is a real boon. Here is a nice, smooth, neat and sensible country; it is so prosperous and respectable. It has no mountains, but in it yawns an abyss of sorrow, of radiance and awesome beauty. This is Rembrandt.

Apart from this, what a contented and matter-of-fact country!

On the Track of the Double-Headed Eagle

Although at this moment nobody is asking me about it, I admit that I am not fond of setting out on a journey; when I am abroad I feel at the mercy of the world, and it is with extreme reluctance, in fact with downright resentment, that I endure all the hardships and complications which, in foreign parts, accompany the simplest of life's activities, such as, for example, the purchase of postage stamps. If, nevertheless, I have undertaken several trips to various regions, it was not because I was particularly inquisitive or adventurous, but through my lack of imagination; you see, when I was put to it, I was unable to think of a passable excuse or pretext to refute the people who, for some reason or other, were prevailing upon me to travel to this place or that. I mention this to show that I have never gone anywhere with particular discoveries in view, or with a hard-and-fast plan, or burdened with expectation, special interest or preconceived theory; as a rule, travelling has overwhelmed me like some species of calamity, unawares and against my will. I should never have dreamt, for example, of looking for tracks of the double-headed eagle; I came across them by chance and with about as much surprise as when I meet a fellow countryman abroad.

So, for example, I was almost scared when, on the threshold of Toledo, at the Bisagra nueva gate, a huge, double-headed eagle, beneath whose pinions a complete roundabout at the very least could have found its way, stretched out its wings above my head. At the first glance this was about as surprising as if I had found the sign of the double-headed eagle on the moon, or the badge of Prague in the excavations of Nineveh. It brought me abruptly face to face with history; with my own eyes I perceived that the Habsburgs held sway over the gates of Toledo, just as they did over the gates of Terezin, alias Theresienstadt.

The next occasion was in Holland; I do not remember exactly where, but it was assuredly some place with a name ending in -dam or -huizen or -kerk or -aar; anyhow, when I was closing my eyes at night, I remembered that in the course of the day I had seen a double-headed eagle on some old building. There you are, I said to myself, then the Habsburgs ruled over Holland, too. Taking it all round, it was a great empire in its time.

But there are things less obvious than badges above gates. For example, in Sicily I never noticed a single badge, but I had a look at the baroque there, and said to myself: why, here in Montreale the baroque looks quite different from what they have up in Italy; it's somehow softer and more gingerbready, more picturesque, more ardent; perhaps it's Spanish influence or something of that sort. And years later I unexpectedly found myself in Spain, looking at Spanish baroque; what I had seen *was* Spanish, but I can't exactly tell in what way; it reminded me of the baroque in Prague and Vienna, Vienna and Salzburg, in fact of Central European baroque in its plastic, picturesque flamboyance and curliness, looseness of build and a sort of architectural romanticism.

Of course, those are Catholic countries; but in Holland I was also constantly being reminded of the same impression; it was a certain flaunting ornateness of the frontages, a sprightly stucco, something ranging between a greater intimacy and a freer phantasy than anywhere else; I should describe it as an out-and-out lack of classicism. In all these countries, dissimilar as they are, certain features glance meaningly at each other; they have a sort of secret in common. In France, in North Germany, in Rome you would search for this in vain; but Sicily and Spain, the Netherlands and Central Europe can look back upon at least a definite common measure of baroque régime. It has left certain inconspicuous but close family traits upon their architectural countenances.

I do not propose, however, to write a chapter about architecture and baroque. All I want to say is, that in countries which at any time have had a joint régime, even though a bad one, you will discover, centuries afterwards, some sort of common intellectual features or traces of such features. Evidently this particular artistic contact was a mere accessory to the political régime; it was brought about by the interchange of people and possessions, it was haphazard and superficial, but there it was.

If the pilgrim finds in so many and such dissimilar countries, the emblem of the Habsburg monarchy, he cannot help realizing the size of that empire, upon which, in good sooth, the sun never set. Bohemia and Hungary, the Alpine lands, Naples, Flanders and the Netherlands, Latin America. And when this is brought home to him in so practical a manner, he can scarcely help reflecting, that it really was conceived on a big scale. The rulers may not have been great; they were cranks and fools, bureaucrats and despots, mediocrities or wily time-servers; certainly not men of great ideas. But not even the historical incapacity or mediocrity of the ruling class can alter the fact that this particular mission was a great one: to turn mediæval Europe into some kind of whole, rising superior to the limits of nationality. It was a baroque attempt to bring about a dynastic Pan-Europe, and in fact more than that—to create, more or less, a league of subject nations. There is no need for us to recall the stupidity and cruelty of this dynastic régime, but if before your very eyes the eagle of Toledo reveals itself as the eagle on the

Prague arsenal, or as any of those other tin
scarecrows which we removed with such
relief a few years back, it startles you, as a
Czech, into a queer realization of how great
a reality and also how great a possibility it
was that those monarchs played ducks and
drakes with. None of us is likely to deplore
the passing of the Habsburg dynasty; but the
greatness and world-wide character of the
empire which our nation, certainly much to
its own detriment, helped to set up, cannot
leave us indifferent, when we encounter its
traces. At all events, it was a great conception of something in the nature of a super-
state. We are not in the least sorry that it
went; but all the same, I think, we might say,
not without political benefit, that this, too,
forms part of our national tradition: not only
the struggle for national self-preservation, but
also the will and ability to fit into a political
order of international scope. It was thus that
we fitted into the Holy Roman Empire; we
fitted into the baroque Habsburg imperium;

historians will be able to tell us whether in both cases it was only the result of compulsion or historical chance or a recurring development of our body politic. I repeat: we have our historical tradition of a share in European politics, more or less broad in its scope and more or less deliberate in its conception. Perhaps this tradition might stand us in good stead to-day.

Of course, it is no longer dynasties or Holy Roman crowns that will shape nations and states into a higher organization and world-order; it will be economic realities, it will be social and humane solidarity, that will one day confer some sort of joint régime upon the mule-drivers of Bisagra, the bulb growers of the polders and those of us who are Czechs to the backbone. It will not be an eagle, but something both more immaterial and more substantial that will give all of us some badge in common. A start is already being made; and it should be an encouragement for us to know, that for our part, we already have some

sort of historical training in such matters. We
are entitled to say: let us take a hand in this;
we've had experience of this kind of thing for
close on a thousand years. We are used to
being in a League of Nations, even though it
wasn't always exactly to our advantage. Perhaps in a way that is what we were meant for.

And here once more I recall those artistic
traces which, to my mind, were to be found
in regions so dissimilar and considerably far
apart. If I was not mistaken in them, if I did
not interpret them altogether wrongly, they
constituted a record, however faulty and im-
perfect, of an intellectual intercourse proceeding from nation to nation along the line
of political contacts. They bore witness to
certain positive and creative values which
accompany an international policy, even
when it is so individual, so forcible and even
contrary to the people's interests as the policy
of the Spanish and Alpine Habsburgs sometimes was. Perhaps it is so, perhaps it would

afford an enormous relief to us or to any
other European people living in the intellectual straits and isolation which we cannot
deny, if above us there were a vaultage of
lines linking us with other nations near and
far, if the new era of life traversed the nervous
systems woven by policy in the organism of
our world. Perhaps hitherto we have not
sufficiently noticed what living sources are
released beneath the historical tread of policy.
If you follow the tracks of the Habsburgs,
you will find, not only baroque, but sundry
other mutual traits; thus, to take only one
instance, the Spanish flamencos by their very
name are connected with the artistic tradition
of old Flanders. Perhaps an ampler world-
order would bring about amongst us and all
other peoples a great deliverance and creative
ardour, a kermesse of the spirit, a Dionysiac
abundance. I believe that it is for international
policy to make the ways and means accessible
to us.

A Small Nation

Not long ago a young Latvian came to see me, and after a few preliminary generalities, blurted out the question which was causing him vital concern: is it worth while to produce a Latvian literature and to publish Latvian books, when only a handful of people can read them? Is it worth the effort to maintain an insulated national entity, and to waste so much energy, merely that the Latvian language should be kept going and a corporate Latvian life should continue? Would it not be wiser to join some larger racial unit and publish books in Russian or German, to share intellectual movements of an ampler scope, and, with a more widely spoken language as instrument, to take an active part in intellectual problems of a European standard?

My dear sir, I said to him, this is familiar ground to us Czechs; some forty years ago a young Czech malcontent, named Hubert Gordon Schauer, was asking the same question. He was soundly abused by the whole nation for his pains, but that, of course, wasn't a final solution of his particular problem. The right answer, it seems to me, is that to-day you come to us from all parts of Europe, including places as far away as Reval, to study such great minds as Březina or Masaryk, and that none of us would dream of bothering his head with the question which to Schauer was a matter of life and death.

'Yes,' said the young man ruefully, 'only I'm not from Reval, but from Riga; Reval is where the Esthonians come from. That just shows you; what can we Latvians signify to the world at large, when everyone mixes us up with the Esthonians or the Lithuanians? Is it really worth while?' And so on.

A Small Nation

Even though Schauer's problem no longer worries us, our position as a small nation causes us trouble in other ways. Some people think that we ought to keep ourselves to ourselves more than most nations do, while others, on the contrary, consider that we should get about in the world to a greater extent; some complain daily of our petty surroundings, while others daily warn us of the big, evil world which is preparing to swallow us up. In short, it is a matter which causes us trouble; and so we are naturally interested to find out how they deal with it in other places where the Lord of Hosts has assigned to the people the same sort of small-scale national undertaking as he has to us. And that—next to Rembrandt—was the first thing I looked for when I went to Holland.

Of course, the Dutch have a slightly exceptional position among the small nations. In the first place, their small country is a big colonial power; for every one Dutchman there are nearly seven brown Javanese,

Malays, and all sorts of pagans producing bananas, copra and sugar-cane. In the second place they have, it seems, enough money and wealth to buy any title of greatness and power, if it should happen to be for sale cheap. But however this may be: no amount of guldens and no amount of overseas colonies will add a single cubit to the stature of this nation numbering not quite eight millions. I do not know whether anyone among them worries his head, as we or the Esthonians (I mean the Latvians) do about the gloomy fate of a small nation; they didn't show any signs of it. What interested me more was to observe how their lack of numbers affects their demeanour and how it comes out in their environment.

It comes out in their environment very plainly and conspicuously, first and foremost in the dimensions of nearly everything that you see there. The Dutch seem to have founded something like a small-scale style of building. Their houses are smaller than anywhere else; the living-rooms are about as tiny and airy as birdcages. Their towns, for the greater part, are so small and compact that you almost feel you could hold them in your hand. Except for the Palace of Peace at the Hague and the Stock Exchange at Amsterdam you will not come across any flamboyant architecture, any impressive bulk, any deviation from the standards of a small country. There is a certain cosiness and frugality with regard to size which, where this nation is concerned, constitute nothing short of an ingrained formal law. And not merely a formal law. I would go so far as to call it a biological one. And even a moral one. Everything that the nation builds and establishes on its small territory is somehow in harmony with the size of the country. Here people do not bite off more than they can chew, by overdoing things either in architecture or in their way of living. They do not pretend to imitate skyscrapers or fun-palaces or

Woolworth buildings; their government offices scarcely differ from the better-class dwelling houses. There is no blatancy, no bumptious and jaunty showing-off, no elephantiasis or exceeding the limits of life-size. At the same time their architecture is among the most progressive; their civil engineers build dams and harbours all over the world. It is not a provincial smallness which sets the standard for the geometry of their lives.

But to come back to what I was saying about the small Dutch buildings. As they do not build too much on a large scale, they are able to make sure that when they do build, they make a neat and thorough job of it. Here they do not use flagstones, but shapely little bricks for building purposes. Here they do not build monumental frontages, but handsome and flawless windows. Their chairs are small and low, but they are nice and cosy to sit on. There is nothing ostentatious to conceal how they are made and what they are made of—namely, good and honest materials. This quality shows the wealth of the nation; but it is a wealth which seems to be divided up into lots of small rations of prosperity. The peasant's cottage looks like a small villa, but so does the workman's dwelling; this neat little house is a tavern, the next one is a greengrocer's shop and the third one is the office of a shipping company. This is standardization with a vengeance, but it is carried out in such a manner that the lower limit of material prosperity is much higher than elsewhere. There is no enormous difference between village, town and city; only the harbours deviate from this attractive level because of their more picturesque social contrasts, but that is how harbours should be.

The word 'level' is most appropriate here. Holland is a small-scale country, but the level which it reaches is high or, at any rate, good. It does not possess any considerable industry, but what industry it has is of high quality. It does not possess an abundance of agricultural soil, but from what soil it does possess it has squeezed out the highest possible standard of production. The foundation of its prosperity is not the sea, but the cows and the polders. They conquer the world with orbs of Eidam cheese and tulip bulbs; but they take these national resources of theirs with a proper seriousness. You ought just to see how fine and effective their milking and gardening activities are, merely to look at. And when you look more into the details, to find out how the thing is done, you will discover there is such stringent control, such scrupulousness and discipline in matters of business and output, such zeal for experiments in breeding, and indeed, such an artistic pride in the excellence of everything produced by the native soil, that you begin to guess the real secret of this small nation. Its strength is in quality. Its national ideal does not aim at sizes but grades. You will discover this in everything: work, way of living, and even in nature itself. If you had to say on the spur of the moment, what the Dutch are distinguished for, you would not think of anything huge, but of the fine, unusual and almost perfect quality of most things which they produce for themselves and also for the world at large. This applies not only to butter, but also to scholarship; not only to narcissus bulbs, but also to workmen's dwellings. The country looks like a toyshop; but the toys are so well made that they never get broken or worn out. To make good, sound articles which will stand plenty of wear is the same as making history.

And here the traveller cannot resist the temptation to generalize just a little: would it not be best for small nations to replace quantity by quality, where ideals are concerned? Would the ability of small nations to compete in the world's fair not best be guaranteed by the special excellence of everything emanating from their factories and shops? They don't need to have a big stock of articles; but what there is should all be flawless. If our shop is small, there's no room in it for trash, rubbish, shoddy and fake. Bad things take up as much room as good ones do, and we haven't got much room to spare.

I do not speak of products, but of something which is more important, viz., ideals. Perhaps we are too ready to assume that we must possess, achieve or produce such and such things entirely by the quantitative standards of world competition. I cannot help feeling that this small nation on the Rhine delta has acted like Mary in the Bible: it has chosen the better part.

www.ingramcontent.com/pod-product-compliance
Lightning Source LLC
Chambersburg PA
CBHW030339020726
47493CB00004B/1334